June 27, 2013

For Joe, artistic,
Keep being
it's the best!

~ Blessings,

Kate

BARN SOUR

Also by Kathleen M. McCann

_____

A Roof Gone To Sky, 2009

The Sea's Rosary, 2008 (chapbook)

The Small Hours, 2008 (chapbook)

BARN SOUR

Poems by Kathleen M. McCann

Cherry Grove Collections

Published by Cherry Grove Collections
P.O. Box 541106
Cincinnati, OH 45254-1106

ISBN: 9781625490209
LCCN: 2013936605

Poetry Editor: Kevin Walzer
Business Editor: Lori Jareo

Visit us on the web at www.cherry-grove.com

Cover photograph by Marcia Ganter
Cover art design by Jean Donohue
Author photograph by Cindy Lou Pelaquin

Acknowledgments

Poems in this collection originally appeared in the following publications:

Big Muddy: "Holly"
Borderlands: "Distant Thunder"
Briar Cliff Review: "Diners Report Seeing Virgin Mary in Food Griddle"
Cape Rock: "The Frost Place, Derry, New Hampshire"
Cider Press Review: "Stain," "Sundered Parts"
Common Ground Review: "The Sea's Rosary"
Eclipse: "In the Gray Morning" (published under the title "Second-Guessing Our Decision to Place My Mother on the Alzheimer's Unit), "As If It Were Yesterday"
The DMQ Review: "From the Window, West Tisbury"
Exit 13: "The Wall, Cloghane"
Four Corners: "After the Rain"
Free Lunch: "Dark Communion"
Grasslimb: "The Figure"
Hidden Oak Poetry Journal: "The Sea This Evening"
Iodine: "Dumb Luck," "Collapse of the Garden"
The Innisfree Poetry Journal: "Wild Roses, Elsberry Cemetery," "The Year We Rang In"
Karamu: "Settling In"
The Kerf: "Crickets"
The Midwest Quarterly: "Fog"
Minnetonka Review: "Hourglass"
Natural Bridge: "The Tinkers, Donegal"
Northeast: "Barn Sour," "Interiors"
Painted Bride Quarterly: "Alzheimer's"
Pembroke Magazine: "Bringing Down the Elms," "After a Nap"
Poetry East: "Past Season," "Saying Thanks," "The Fight Within"
Solo: "When The Heart Decides to Bear Itself Away"
South Carolina Review: "Dorothea Lange's Young Migrant Worker, California, 1936"
South Dakota Review: "Lone Egret"
The Texas Review: "The Hallway"

Timber Creek Review: "The Three-Legged Dog"
Visions International: "The Caretaker's Instructions"
Witness: "Mullagh," "Sky Comes to Ground"
White Pelican Review: "Sitting Tight in February"
Xavier Review: "Troubles"

In memory of my mother and father

The past beats inside me like a second heart.

                                    - John Banville

~

     ...the little that we get for free,
the little of our earthly trust. Not much.
About the size of our abidance with the cows,
 the iris, crisp and shivering, the water
still standing from spring freshets,
the-yet-to-be-dismantled elms, the geese.

                              - Elizabeth Bishop

Table of Contents

I. Other Winters, Old Suns

II. Interiors

III. Day Labor

IV. In the Gray Morning

V. Ash

છ છ છ છ છ છ

I

Other Winters, Old Suns

Holly

Teach to me what's been forgot.

- Anne Minogue, Harpist

To notch the cycles of the moon
our ancestors carved bone.
The fierce drive for knowledge
red as these tight berries,
pea-sized promise of throaty
stories – the gone by.
No roads to interrupt the eye,
only far fields, meadowlands
unlatched to gorse, loosestrife, birdsong.
Bring them up to the ear, -
if you must, shake them,
cupped in the palm.
Slice the skin of the bright bead in your palm.
Listen: other winters, old suns.

The Fight Within

Look how the field takes on light
this time of day,
how the grass drinks sunlight.
Smell the rain in the air,
a faint drizzle to come.

You can beat this dog
till blood oozes from its hide.
You will never break him.
Put down the mitt. Drop your arms
to your side, your tired head to the chest.

Let go the fight within and listen...
for the breath's catch, your own cry.

Night Sounds

Always the clanging pipes,
the rustle of cat and dog.
Rocking in the old chair,
I hear my house sounds.

Tonight, a faint hum
in the air, a thin whistle
from the high heat:
strangers, house and I,

given to staying together,
learning
in the shared compartmented air
the necessity of humming.

Hourglass
One can never consent to creep when one feels an impulse to soar.
Helen Keller

Even the most pedestrian moments:
a broken fingernail, the time taken
to unsnag one's sweater from a thorn,
keep the Icarus in us all earthbound.
Another day, well spent, spent.
Time is offered up on its own altar.

Those at the bottom, blinded by sun
and dizzying effects of the mountain's height,
go home where they lock the door to pray.
Fervent, unfettered prayer:
for wisdom, fast feet:
and that flung wish, home.

The Figure

What would it mean
if meaning to find ourselves,
we found ourselves?

A back road, the country
night full of nothing
but moon and starlight

and a shadowy figure
way up the road
waving,

hand outstretched
as we approach,
trying to pass

untouched.

Lone Egret

Classically stagy, goose-neck
elegant, river's third eye.
Pencil thin head. S
for a throat. Skeleton of a saint.

Plodder, preening posturer.
One foot,
another.
Up from the dank weeds.

Distant Thunder

Dismal cowl above our heads, drab
funk, color of the depressive's mood.
A tame sky gives in
to the unannounced rupture of mid-day,
an inner life as stark as this blanched template.
Lightning from afar, another crack of thunder.
Then rain leaves room for nothing.

Haunts

At the shoreline this morning
horseshoe crabs lie coupling, bubbling
breath, knuckling one atop the other.
Shell knocks shell, gravelly scrapes.
One lies pressed among stones at the shallow,
sunk by the weight of the other, raw desire,
an urge to root, to close the eyes
and never move nor lift the head again.

A noise like a shoe scuffed against the floor;
attached still, they turn.
Seasoned to this coastline, strictured haven,
yet willing to push out, then let the bottom go
and move along the current once more
into deeper, more formidable waters,
cold and deep, and carrying the inevitable
uncoupling to sequestered haunts.

Lilacs

Like dry weeds,
dust in the hand,
the lilacs remain.
Button-tight, bled dry
of hue, crinkled effigy
of what was.

The mower drones on
in the long grass. May
with its delicacies,
summer's assault
far off; yet with us now,
day's trickster moon.

Whatever we love
remains. Pinwheels,
once violet and white, turn
inward on their long stems,
as if for the strength
to come again.

And

Bridge-builder. Saddled with history's trek,
set in motion
made to carry more; always more. Pack animal.
Never the lesser load.

Immodest little word.
Shimmering errant knight,
crusader staring fearlessly
into the mapped out world.

II

Interiors

From the Window, West Tisbury

In the marginalia of this day
the leaves write themselves
in. Gone the green grass.

A loose-flapped blue tarp,
careless old throw,
drapes its wood.

After a Nap

Once more the world a canvas
anchored by fresh stamina.
The dog will get a bath, the vase
flowers from the evening walk.
In due time.

Now the familiar floats back:
a sweater's sleeve grazing the floor,
the cherished bookcase with its stubborn nicks,
photographs – their long sweep –
people, pets, the past.

Tempered hook, our disquiet
but faithful past. Who among us
has such forbearance?
We turn from our blurry brink
to hope this day's hinge will hold.

The Three-Legged Dog

That's the way to fly.
So sure of itself, low and effortless,
a lone cormorant skimming the sea's surface.
The weather mild for this time of year,
unseasonable, we New Englanders say.
Under full sun the morning drifts; the ease
of a barely perceptible tide inches in,
up close, an old friend wanting all
of you; your time, your attention, your love.

From the house on the top of the hill,
the woman will come down with her dog
and cross the boulevard for the day's walk.
The slow sweet sidestep away from concern.
Out on the tide.
And the dog, as adept with three as with four,
will take his legs over the rocks and sand,
will smell once more the briny salt of home.
A rippling cage of possibility
within those broad flanks; an effortless
unassailable urge.

A day's tally: bits of bone, shard, full sun
and warm breeze, the sea's rub and run of stones
into the day's lap.

Free

Drooping and barely legible after three
days of rain, the oak tag sign
stands by its giveaway: two chairs,

rusted-to-ruin-cast-offs
brought up from the cellar
and put by the side of the road.

Sad old mutts, shoulder to shoulder
the undignified pair with matching
tear in the black upholstered seats

tease the eye of the passerby.
A quick peek of cotton fleck,
the color of surrender, cries

Uncle! For all
that is cumbersome,
cornered,

let go.

Diners Report Seeing Virgin Mary in Food Griddle

Of course one can't get beans or breakfast now.
The news has reached the mob and muscled mass
who crowd in hopes to glimpse the Virgin's bow,
or other moves, perhaps a bit more crass.

There's nothing like the theatre of the real.
One day a cook, the next a checkered seer
who holds the griddle high: the day's best deal.
This pancaked miracle, mirage, so dear.

No one will clean the grille, disturb the face
that came the day the wrestlers did to town,
to bulk and buckle in the swap meet's pace,
and claim this chit of border town's renown.

Calexico, chin-up, hold tight your fame.
To you, Our Lady of Guadalupe came.

Wyeth's Distant Thunder

Two pines pitch thin shadows
over the ferns, an occasional
daisy. The air still.

Berries picked, coffee drunk,
binoculars set aside.
Betsy's hands rest atop
her blue shirt.
Felt hat, a shade for the eyes.

Rattler, the old hound, first
to bolt at a twitch of thunder,
peeks out from his hill of bed,
eyes down for the count, ears
shut tight against his head.

How tired these two grow
on a perfect summer day.
Nothing troubles.

Monday's Hair Cut
for Bob at Salvation Army's Day Care

I need ten dollars…ten dollars,
mantra-pinched face, worry
palmed only at Bob's prompt beep.
Up inside the van, with a host
of lost faces to ride among,
she cradles the dingy purse
belonging to her mother,
its stash of Kleenex, bobby pins,

and ten dollar bill
death-gripped in the lap
for the mind to pour over,
lips to mutter…*is this all?*
Then thought gives way
to new thoughts,
a flutter of birds
crossing her face.

The Frost Place, Derry, New Hampshire

Summer's gone with its seasonal visits
and left the front door's hale & hearty
green, the lure of one life, to welcome.
Through the kitchen window…
the Glenwood's deep squat,
a last bouquet on a table ringed
by chairs sturdy in age (home-made?)

If you were here, sprawled
among this couple with their baby
and dog, grass rife with apples' decay,
might you fend off
any broodish thoughts,
say…the darkening of year,
and make a stay?

Bringing Down the Elms

Mrs. Sargent lived there. House
of mystery for the neighborhood's children.
Summer evenings, nurse Lucy took her charge
and the old bull-dog out to the sidewalk's end.
Coolidge Avenue's motley group: timid Lucy
with her head down, old Sarge with his
blood-bold eyes & droopy ass,
and the invalid, cropped hair rimmed
with a broad white bandage, right-hand splayed
on a splint and bandaged, also.
Shading with her good hand
eyes that couldn't see (or so she said),
she scanned the street.

Iced coffees rattle on deaf ears.
Pulleys and ropes bounce the bucket man
up, then down until he finds and feeds
a next limb to the gassy machine,
its blade spewing chips that drop through
the air, flinty fields of confetti.
From the upstairs window I watch
my mother's lips moving, head shaking
her blue hat to the grass, the one place
dementia hasn't reached, her rhythmic rows
cut to a precise slant.
Gert's little Fenway, the neighbors,
who bunch against the long fence, call it.

In a cloud of noise, the elms come down.
All afternoon…eyes on the spectacle.
No one leaves.

Strands of words drop like stone.
A premonition of autumn
in the air and on the mouth.

Troubles

Sorry for your troubles – the Irish
whistle through tight teeth.

A sack of spoiled spuds,
dismal weather, stray

dog toweled off in the hall,
welcomed in.

Troubles? What
are they but trifle

next to bone-bred
havoc.

Mullagh

Sheep and water and walls.
Lichen – so much the eyes hurt
catching on its white,
as far as these hills allow.

Once a village lived
within these close-walled lanes:
tenders for the fields, ears to hold birdsong,
eyes, the black of Peddler's Lake.

Dark and deep this corrie lake,
glacier formed. Dark hides deep.

* Mullagh means hidden in Gaelic

The Tinkers, Donegal

The pup is flapdoodle happy,
belly rubbed by the boy
with the far-off stare, mud-creased face.

Tarp and tack and roadside tin.
A truck, a used-to-be if ever it
ran, sprawls in disrepair.

Two girls stir a clothesline as they step through
a flurry of cloth diced in squares, dried rags.
They wear smocks cut from feed cloth,

burlap sacks that swim on their bones –
skinny minnies starched with pride's faint lip curl.
Want gleams like a fishhook in the sun.

Interiors

What taste to decorate with such intent.
Who meant for the china's blue edge
to sink teeth into dinner parties prepared
with perfect light for illuminating these walls?
She could not have foreseen this, the color
already here from the first walk through,
cool crisp blue, breezy not cold,
faintly formal, not stiff.
The white candles with their tightly sprigged
floral scene, blue of course, would brighten
any room, make a perfect border
if not already ordained as candles
adding a touch on each side of the long
gold mirror, not too much.
The Indian print with its blue-plum parade
will never march past its black frill, never
climb down and run from the sideboard.
Even the decanter's interior looks blue,
squat duck, six baby shot glasses in tow
holding down the madras print, positioned
across from the pitcher with its oval
scene: two bluebirds on a branch, background blue.
The whole world is blue, if you look for it.
Faint stripe in the chair, a tablecloth,
the dishes in the sink, the sink.

The Year We Rang In

Maybe five years a stay-at-home by then,
a young woman with enough pills
for two in the pocket, a sadness
that could check the sea.

Nana wants to watch Lawrence Welk,
the usual for her Saturday night, why not,
so it's New Year's?
There will be others.

But tonight, it is just the two of us,
flesh and blood, cold comfort shared,
thing we do that is remembered
long after she is gone.

It was she who said, *get a pan and a spoon,*
when the ball descended in New York.
She, who opened the front door to the coal sky,
banging the spuds pan through the burly cold.

And then I, banging and banging and banging,
forgetting how inextricably bound
by the 'Irish mood' we were,
murdering our cold drum.

Dark Communion

The first December snow.
Five months beyond your death.
Like one more ritual to purge July,
I throw my window wide, give my parlor
to the chill of inrushing flakes.
Wafers on my tongue, the dark's communion.
Now there is only the cold and the cold.

Dorothea Lange's Young Migrant Worker, California, 1936

Cracked and scarred, her coat
hangs from her like an old buffalo hide.
On that bowed face, beneath bowl-cut
bangs and a gaze that looks past
nothing, shame's imprimatur.

Dirt in the corners of sleepy-
seed eyes, the neck's crease,
the scabs on her legs and
the dingy cape cradling
one shoulder like a sling.

Her toes press down hard
through their flimsy shoes,
but her cotton sack
catches daylight.

And the picking fields wait.

III

Day Labor

Saying Thanks

I kneel to smell
a low-to-the-ground
beach plum.
This is church-like,
worship the real.

A light breeze wafts.
Overhead, a gull becomes
a wireless show, pulled
across the bluest heaven
way, way up.

Oh, say thank you.
The breath of this
pink flower centers me.

Precious life
stops me still.

Boys in a Pasture

- Winslow Homer

High sun warms their backs,
bare feet to dab the air,
flex the toes.
The feel of grass
between thumb and finger,
chores back home
beyond the fence posts.
Confident in their broad-cloth
shirts & wide-brimmed hats,
our boys.
Life is good inside their pastoral locket,
buttoned-down in history.

Wild Roses, Elsberry Cemetery

Your petals drop in excess onto stone.
Each spring this royal crimson down the rows,
Through rain or sun toward elemental bone.

This morning in the air a fuss of crows
Takes umbrage at the way you let all go;
Rebukes as well the one who comes and mows,

Caring no less for crows than petals' show.

Sitting Tight in February

Dreaming you
up and down at night
tires me out.
Like the flames, leaping &
licking themselves to death
in the stove at night,
I'm exhausted.

How will it be
that I begin to move
away from you?
Simply, like sunlight
backing out of a room
in late afternoon.

Perhaps this summer
after a heavy allowance of time
I'll find my way
down your way.

Hold you.
Whisper back
where it belongs

one year's worth
of the gone by.

Crickets

    — *a May evening, Bartlett, New Hampshire*

Compact voices, *chorus*
too mild a word
for the hard labor

they do – must,
for this forged song

to split the evening
in two: the then and now

of again.

Sky Comes to Ground

Gone with its lavish
tinctorial surge,
Dingle's Water Company's rainbow,
the backdrop.

Sky comes to ground and nothing
holds. Dingle's clouds thin –
thin and disperse.
Warmth on the back slips,

a hand drawn away.

February Thaw

All night
the cats lick
themselves in.
The dog sprawls,
paws twitching,
running somewhere.
This morning old snow
goes down to water.

Clamming on St. Paddy's Day

Bent so long he is stone.
Loner. Fixed point on the horizon.
All the others cash in close,
baggy-benders raking low-tide.
Not him.
Mythic figure, too far out to work.
The mud his boots must own, long
over the top and down to grease his toes.
Pinpoint the eye tracks through sunlight,
where is he now?
Gone where the hours have ended.
Through the slat of a day, showered, freshly clothed
and seated at his designated stool, he downs one,
then another. One more –
for the Irish Saint, for day's disappearance.

Sunrise in Eastport

On the roof of the old Wass sardine factory
two gulls strain to outdo each other.
Churling gutturally, reaching,
like two boys in a spitting contest.

Everywhere else the day wakes.
A pink comes on thin & thick at once,
as if someone shoots the hue
from a cannon off Canada's side.

Or squeezes it from a tube,
sleight-of-hand behind Cherry Island,
spurting it up &
out all over us.

Faith

calls our name above the bushes, brambles,
riprap of lives: despair,
a snake at the throat,
bright heights, the world awaiting our harvest.

Faith, full of permutation, calling and
calling and calling, like the whippoorwill's
plaint deep in the woods becomes its own call.
Braced by hope a lamenter's lean note strikes.

Letting Go

Trees practice it.
Don't fault them.

There's one like silver, you say.
A whirligig of leaf slices air.

Your eyes are what I find.
Their blue stuns.

Beneath me on the blanket
a voice halts...

look where I look,
feel what I feel.

Day Labor

Early Saturday mornings, weaving up
city side streets, flinging advertisements
pinned inside a thin elastic band.
Good aims, each one.

Boozers, little
or no excuse.
Sun comes up,
day ends in a y.

One more toss till break.
A few guys huddle for a smoke &
quick count of fliers left.
Sometimes they trash them,
most times they don't.

Toughing it out,
two more streets.
Going, going,
gone.

Quitting time,
the bar.

Cedar-Tree Neck Sanctuary, Martha's Vineyard

Unseasonably mild, and the day
conspires to pass its plenty on:
it is Thanksgiving.
The breeze makes light of the air;
handles the reeds with the faintest rattle
in their willowy throats.
Bittersweet arrests the eye.
Gray granite smooth with warmth,
from our promontory the sea watches us.
No need for photographs. The day ~
its own tableaux stretching the woods…
three old friends down
                rung
                    after

                        rung

to the beach where the dogs run
and the new pup forgets
all commands. So new
this horizoned world.
What can he do
but drink from a tub so vast?

Infirm

In the days given
she turns inward
beyond boredom,
a place few inhabit.
None walk.
The cuckoo interrupts

a drowse: one o'clock,
two, or three.
Dust motes down
and down,
a soundless
graze of curtains.

Dumb Luck

You open the drawer, to a paper cut.
Sudden prick, the slivered slice, deep enough.

The car will not start, first day of the job.
The cellar floods, with you that far away.

The hours scatter like birds from the fields
shorn from our lists: poor lessons in everything.

An August Sky, New England

This evening's sky sets out a feast.
Prelude: the calligrapher's faint
firm strokes, understated.

A perfect ~ pause ~
until the platters wheel by
on invisible carts.

Quarried marble missives;
deep-veined, blue
on blue, earth's

first hue.

IV

In the Gray Morning

The Caretaker's Instructions
-Mount Hood, Brookline

Rust-colored pine needles pad
ground steeped in its own repose.
The dogwoods are in full splendor.
Lilacs inch toward brown, threads
of color plucked from their veins
like purple popsicles in the heat.
Crows caucus in the high pines,
custodians of their own noise.

The caretaker's careful instructions
prepare the way. Up in back,
deep in the far corner, lies a grandmother
who was as grave as this ground.
Partial to none, fixed
on the hard task of living,
loveless.
Dogwoods shower the ground with petals.
The saucy crows talk back.

When the Heart Gives Out

On the last day of his life my father
descended the stairs for a simple breakfast
of toast and coffee. Not much kitchen talk
with a tee time waiting, foursome buddies
who, if they are lucky like my father
and have a wife, kiss her; then with dishes
in the sink, leave, as he did to cross town.
A dizzying September day, the kind of day
that would make anyone, not just the lucky,
glad to be alive, sun warming the bones,
the spirit. A day for all the living.

Three days later, coming from the cemetery,
we pass the course and ask the driver to stop.
A golfer himself, he willingly swings in, jokes
he'll make Monday's tee time while he waits.
My mother places one rose on the first hole.
One red beacon, brave little suitor.
All day her pinned and private nosegay
flaps and lunges in the wind, even
as it stays put. All day through the bright air
clubs drive our blessings and our burdensome
anger beyond reach.

Barn Sour

in memory of my father

Remember the old Saturday morning westerns,
a dozen from Dunkin Donuts, and three
pajama-ed kids holding down time?
You could poke a hole through the sagging brown
weave beneath the TV's screen, but we never did;
only allowed our fingers to come away
fresh with RCA's silver stuck to them.
Extract all shoot-em- up, yip yipping loud
too long cowboy slinging bluff slash bravado,
and what are you left with?

It is what we left that rings in our ear:
an old-fashioned living room, modest
but ample; a child's holster on the arm
of the couch, outfitted cowgirl, beaming.
On the back porch, a mother and her mother
talk with a friend; father's doing a double.
The apple trees, bent with fruit, are thriving.
Somewhere a horse balks, resists its rider,
fights to turn back. *Barn sour,* my friend who knows
them terms it, poor beasts who strain, who so ache.

Onslaught

She has scoured her calendar
all morning: *what day is it?*
Her mind is the tide,
always leaving.
An island

is no poorer for lack
of use. Only a foreign
shore, a dreamy place
never rowed toward.
Yet always there.

Alzheimer's

Underneath the late day sun
hell-bent reeds hijack her voice.
Sentences – pelted bullets –
dissolve in easterly wind.
Sticks, splintered reeds, afternoon,

gone. All thoughts soon forgotten,
falling away, detritus.
No notation, no notch for time,
like salt's fresh line slashing marsh,
fierce in delineation.

Here, no further. Mark this mark.
Tomorrow's another day.
She calls for the dog's return.
Then words, trampled by more words,
fan out in the woods, like smoke.

In the Gray Morning

for my mother

A gull keens the weight
of the world. So early

in the gray morning,
the smell of sea

at the door. Last night
I dreamt a young girl

bundled tight, her mother
pulling her sled

up Wilson Avenue.
Roosevelt, Taft, Harding

covered in fresh snow.
Jingle bells, jingle bells

the mother sings
and sings and sings

all the way home.

Keening for 74 Coolidge

All night
incessant rain
rattles the old panes.
This is her home,

bed-bound lady of #202,
in the lap of departure.
Put your ear to her lips
and listen...

home.

Elegy

This morning heavy rain
crawls the cellar, pools in dim
corners of neglect
beneath the foundation's burred
blur, grizzled blotch
of hump-backed stone
seeping cold.
Nothing held back.

One Wish

in memory of Teresa

Catalogues arrive like snow;
usurp your parents' mailslot,
daily hits. Women with great teeth
shelter children in full shots of the latest –
best parkas – ice dabbed collars, -
vintage Flexible Flyer a propped prop,
clever peek at cow skin gloves
plush with double-stitched fingers
and the firm brown grain that sells
us our toughness.

On J. Jill's cover a woman – scant lipstick,
wisp of lilac on the eyes, hair swept back –
dreams good dreams on a jailer's striped pillow.
Groomed look, right arm bent for the cameras,
lower half slipped under to cradle
our pretty woman's face.
Like a brazen L, this arm in its blueberry
blue popcorn sweater cries out at us
that it is almost Christmas. Damn it;
buy.

Small, But a Loss

Again today the tide buries the reeds
when we arrive to find the chair missing.
Lucky for the dogs, no moral compass
to spoil this summer day, high tide's intent.
Tails high, they head in. No fuss or fore-thought,
no need for incremental submersion.
What's here is theirs and here is to be had.
Not one whit for the beach chair, not one glance
around, stray thought as to its whereabouts.
No urge to scour beyond the cedar tree
where it lay folded and put away.
Why does the mind struggle so to say *gone?*
Rather choke back the formed words than pronounce
the grave; as well, the inconsequential.

When the Heart Decides to Bear Itself Away

It will leave you when you least expect it.
No need to prepare, lay out clothes, primp,
or look in the mirror one last time.
Never in a million years, later thoughts.
And yet not the slightest traceable hint.
At least a thousand times let it be said
how it means to do the disappearing.
No fandango, no line dancing with other
over-fifties. No Hully Gully.
Nothing fancy,
just gone.

The Sea's Rosary

Nothing gold can stay.

–Robert Frost

Marsh grass, gold plumes fanning the air, so hot
it breaks a sixty-nine year old record.

The old adage – records are made to break.
Yet the core of this day a honed litany:

the tennis ball the dog won't let go of
except for another long sea-ward launch.

The red chair, low to the ground and empty,
while the woman who loves to swim, swims.

High tide's prayerful retreat, bead on bead,
the sea's rosary, saying itself away.

V

Ash

After the Rain

Look at these stalks
unable to stand, punch drunk,

bullied into submission,
bent backward.

What can we learn?
Of time taken,

hour after sweet hour
for weeks now.

The gardener's modest wants,
whispered to the evening.

And when the flowers come,
as certain they will,

more lessons, these
rock hard.

Settling In

Summer dismantled, cottage shuttered.
And the old dog sleeps on. Oblivious
to sea air, a mower at the window.
Labor Day's pack-up business.

No pain with his head in a square of sun,
legs that take him anywhere in slumber.
Sleep, Benson. Sleep so long you wake as wind
snapping the rose hips back.

Fog

The morning fog presses in on us.
Dew clings to the deck's rail
where a lone drop took hours to fall.

Hardly noteworthy. Small potatoes
in the planet's mix and whirl.
Yet, a loss; a slippage as slight as this,

noted. Something that caught the eye,
gone. Gone – that bully of a word – railing
and ringing. Usurper, nothing spared.

Collapse of the Garden

The season has brought forth its work to bury.
Nothing left to tend.
The birds insist on remnant,
the ghost of petal fall.
They swell the naked trees,
sweep the dismal ground.
Stubborn desire; a will to extract
what little from dearth.
Callous earth receives its stark remainder:
toppled stalks rouged by sea air, nut hard
vestige of bud, brown coils wound
button tight.

Past Season

> *Who wants to love forever. Love should fall*
> *like the apple blossom, die at the kiss*
> *of a bee, learn to perish, come to an end.*
> — Rebecca Seiferle

In a twist of roots,
the spread and gnarl of seed
and vine, the garden slides
toward disrepair.

No one to tend the withered rows,
walk amongst the rub and whistle
of stalks. Nor smell the whiff
of potato below.

An empty vessel,
is all.

The Sea in Late October

A Keatsian season of mist
and brine.
Upturned blue-bottomed dinghies line
the seawall where a worker's hands
scrub loose – barnacles, sea-weed, sand –
hoist each boat to its roped bed
high in the yacht club's rafters.

Ever mindful of the harsh night to come,
the wind's interminable moan and bite,
waves borne daily to this portioned world.
The shining flickering cast of waves
affixed to destination's star.
Kindled from an ancient source,
the sea offers its fierce-tongued fables.

Heron in the Reeds

Gone before binoculars meet the eye.
Muted wriggle, blue-black
hint of haste across a page.
Disappearance so slick
the evening's pink lets go.

Grief

The long autumn days bleed
with a beauty seldom matched.

The woods accept all
offerings, be they sudden

or slow.
Whatever must,

falls.

Ash

Burnished gold, hallowed
red, green's fiery rope
up moss to mountain,
slips from our grasp.
Do not weep, the dying

grass sings in our sleep.
At dawn wing beats.
Goodbye bright October,
bone-searing drenched wool
smell, ash.

Great Esker Park, Mid-Winter

The marsh grass bends
back against the bank,

long full hair brushed
with the head down.

Ice interrupts, damming any vestige
of life in the rum-gold grass.

All is forgotten: fall, summer's long lean.
Nothing but silence.

Old Hand

It's worse as one ages,
though wisdom has it reversed.
Nothing to do but move on, find
one's feet, collect one's senses,
start over again.

Go and you will get there.
Neither the lie nor the trouble.
Each time rebuilding,
red bricks thinner and thinner
until they pass through our hands like water.

Watering the Roses by the Cellar Door

How long their red will climb
New England's skies, unknown.

One sees father
and daughter in the yard,

early evening: digging,
watering, tending to.

Her sisters found no joy
in tools or dirty nails.

Unlike her, the tomboy,
missing son, she said.

Old roses, may your red
forever claw

and keep this cellar door,
crane west toward that –

bloodache, New England's
staunch sky.

The Hallway

in memory of Aunt Ann

A spool of thread never moved
from the crenellated umbrella stand;
no takers for needlework.
Not my aunt, diminutive dynamo,
chain smoking through thrift stores
and yard sales and Friday night auctions
all over the South Shore.
Any place her hands might find
and feel *good wood:* ash, black oak,
mahogany, the sought after substantive
touch, warm like lamb's wool to the cheek.

Housework could always wait
and did. Dust motes adrift,
down and down
through the hallway's taper of light…
narrow
reach for the stoic stand
and its green spool,
the antique clock
unwound and dumb.

The Wall, Cloghane

Over the lichen's white dabs, the velvet press
of moss, a spray of grass fans out.

How long has it seeded and prospered there,
like an old broom's stray strands?

Part and parcel of the fallen down farm,
holding out, a lament for all that was,

the hand extended for its glove, long lost.

Stain

Rain ticks the house, over
original shingles long covered
by siding. Every third year
my father hip-nudged the ladder.
Summer business: hunter green stain.
For weeks the ladder lay with splotched
rags on the side lawn all night,
until the next morning's shimmy
and tug, pulleys and ropes.

Cast in a pearl of fog, neighboring
houses hide behind lanterns
and the solace of first hours.
No one has uncurled the newspaper
from its blue plastic sheath.
Nor learned that an infant
hurled against bedrails has died.
The walled cuckoo unleashes its bridled tongue:
            Is so!... Is so!... Is so!

Sundered Parts

I shoot at night because nothing stands in for life better than a lit window.
                                    –Joe Johnson

Early sky as meek as beach glass.
Within the hour a storm gathers
rippling the grass like a pond,
the luxury of stasis washed away.
Give and take; the history of the world.

By afternoon the birds are back.
For a while such light as never
before. The kitchen window fans out
to shimmering fruit, a tree trunk
pocked with rain.

Who would know, past nightfall,
what to record of this one day?
The yard is quiet except for crickets.
Inhabitants of the house have gone to bed.
Someone forgets the kitchen light.

The Sea This Evening

Lilacs come across town on the wind.
There is a foretaste of rain on the brine.
A pram, battered to heartbreak blue, sets up
against a powdering wall.

Hold onto the world. If not for comfort,
for an evening's surety; salt on the tongue
and the bell of nightfall ringing.

As If It Were Yesterday

Tomorrow will come
with its handful of snow
or full course.
Forecasters be damned.
Bearers of bad roads,
schedules undone.

In the early morning light,
from memory's bright purse,
Fore River's steep crane lords
over ship yard workers carding
in at the gate, lunch pails &
thermos tucked, wool caps snug.

And the collie…
asleep on the back stoop
beneath the peeling *Esso*
beyond the rotary &
its rotund granite ball.

Fifty years, like that.

Kathleen M. McCann teaches poetry and American literature at Eastern Nazarene College in Quincy, Massachusetts. An ordained minister in the United Church of Christ, she has served small rural churches in the past, both in Massachusetts and Missouri. Her poems have appeared in many small presses, such as *The Threepenny Review; Eclipse; The Midwest Quarterly; Witness; South Dakota Review; Natural Bridge; Poetry East*. New poems are forthcoming in *Rhino; Blackbird;* and *CRANNOG*, Galway, Ireland. Presently she is looking for a home for *Sail Away The Plenty*, a full-length collection of poems about the Irish famine and its imprint on spirit, body, and mind.

CPSIA information can be obtained at www.ICGtesting.com
Printed in the USA
BVOW031257180413

318110BV00002BA/35/P